Spotter's Guide to
SEA & FRESHWATER
BIRDS

Joe Blossom

Illustrated by
Trevor Boyer & Alan Harris

Contents

Some of the colour illustrations in this book have been previously published in the Spotter's Guide to Birds also published by Usborne.

The illustration on page 1 shows Red-breasted Mergansers during their courtship display.

Edited by Karen Goaman

Designed by Anne Sharples

Cover illustration by Deidre Morgan

Additional illustrations by
Tim Hayward and Sally Burrough

First published in 1981 by
Usborne Publishing Limited
20 Garrick Street, London WC2

© 1981 by Usborne Publishing Limited

Printed in Great Britain

How to use this book

This book will help you to identify most of the birds to be seen by the sea, on estuaries, marshes, rivers, lakes, reservoirs, streams and ponds. Birds of freshwater places are found on pages 6–31 and sea birds on pages 32–48. Groups of birds are shown together, so sea ducks appear with the other ducks and a few waders of freshwater places are found with the other coastal waders.

The **illustrations** show the birds standing, swimming, perching or flying, depending on how the bird is most often spotted.

There are separate pictures of the females (♀ means female) if they are very different from the male (♂ means male). If a bird's summer and winter plumage are very different, both kinds of plumage are usually shown.

The **description** next to each bird tells you where it may be seen and its size. A bird is measured from the tip of its beak to the tip of its tail (see diagram). Birds on the same page are not always drawn to scale.

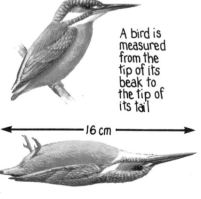

A bird is measured from the tip of its beak to the tip of its tail

◄——— 16 cm ———►

The description also tells you if the bird is seen in Britain only at certain times of the year. If no season is mentioned it means that the bird is generally present in Britain all year. Information about where a bird is found usually refers to Britain. So if the description says that a bird breeds only in East Anglia, this does not mean it does not breed elsewhere in Europe.

Each time you spot a bird, tick it off in the small circle next to the bird's illustration.

The **Scorecard** at the back of the book gives a score for each bird. A very rare species scores 25 points and a common one 5 points. At the end of a day out spotting you can add up your total score. As some of the birds are rare in Britain, you can tick off rarer species if you see them in a wildfowl collection, zoo or bird garden.

Areas covered by this book

This book can be used to identify birds all over Europe. The birds shown in the book will not necessarily be found in every European country. If a bird is very rare in Britain, the description will tell you so. Look out for it if you go abroad.

Watching sea and freshwater birds

These birds are often easier to spot since many live out in the open on water or on shores.

When you can name many of the species (types of birds) you may want to find out more about them. There is a list of books to read and clubs to join at the end of the book. The identification guides suggested will help you with any difficult or rare species.

Where to go

Here are some unusual places to look for sea and freshwater birds:

▲ Flooded gravel pits and reservoirs as well as lakes are good for wildfowl, especially in winter.

▲ Sea birds, waders and a few wildfowl may be watched from the promenade or foreshore.

Take care when out birdwatching. Don't climb sea cliff faces or walk close to the edge of cliff tops to look at nesting birds. You may fall or knock loose stones down and frighten the birds from their nest.

Mudflats on estuaries with tides are also dangerous. Keep to the hard shoreline unless you are with an adult who knows the area and the times of the tides.

▲ School playing fields often attract gulls and some kinds of waders.

Keeping records

Keep a notebook for recording the different birds you can see. Write down the place, date, time of day, weather conditions and state of the tide if this is relevant. Describe any birds whose names you don't know, making rough sketches with colour notes to help you identify them later.

Helpful things to look for

Size: Is it bigger or smaller than a Pigeon or Starling?

Colours? Including beak and legs, and any special markings

Posture: When standing is it upright or more horizontal?

What is it doing? Swimming, diving, wading, perching or walking?

Note or sketch comparative *lengths* of body, neck, head, legs and tail

IN FLIGHT
Note or sketch any colours or markings on wings and rump

If neck is long, is it extended or held folded back?

If legs are long, do they trail out behind when taking off or in flight?

Equipment

As you become more interested in birdwatching, you will find that a pair of binoculars are a great help in spotting and identifying birds.

The best sizes are 8 × 30 or 8 × 40. Never choose a magnification (the first figure) of more than 10 since with these you will find it difficult to hold the picture still for long, particularly in a strong wind. When buying binoculars, go to a good dealer and explain that you want them for birdwatching.

When you become even more experienced, a telescope can prove useful for sea bird watches and wader spotting at greater distances. Ask an experienced birdwatcher for help and advice before buying a telescope.

Parts of a bird

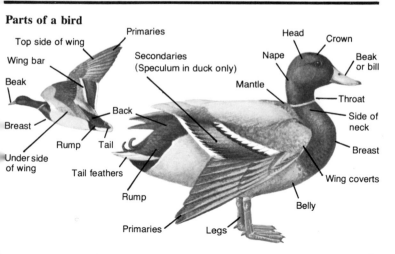

Top side of wing
Primaries
Wing bar
Secondaries (Speculum in duck only)
Beak
Back
Breast
Rump
Tail
Under side of wing
Tail feathers
Rump
Primaries
Legs

Head
Crown
Nape
Beak or bill
Mantle
Throat
Side of neck
Breast
Wing coverts
Belly

5

Swans

Mute Swan

Seen all year in Britain on rivers and lakes. Also common in town parks. Builds huge mounded nest on islets in freshwater and marshes. Its long neck enables it to feed on water plants in deep water. Normally silent but if irritated hisses or gives a snorting grunt. 152 cm.

All species of swan fly with neck stretched out

In flight, wing beats make a regular swishing-whistle noise

Juveniles keep grey-brown plumage until they are three years old

Juvenile

Adults have orange bill with black knob

Neck curved in S-shape

The downy young of all species of swan are called cygnets

Cygnets are sometimes carried on the backs of the adult when swimming

Swans

Bewick's Swan ▶

Smallest of the swans, with the shortest neck. Breeds in the Russian Arctic. Most winter in southern half of Britain and Ireland. Pattern of yellow on. bill varies. 122 cm.

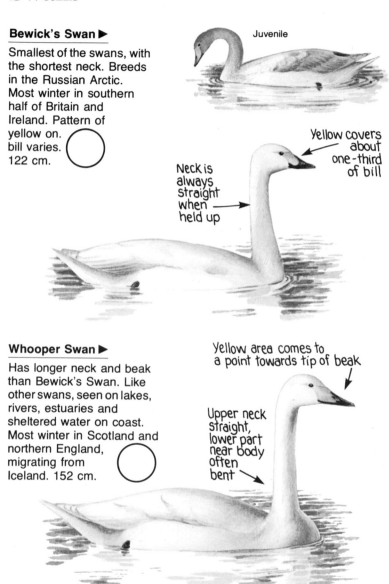

Juvenile

Yellow covers about one-third of bill

Neck is always straight when held up

Whooper Swan ▶

Has longer neck and beak than Bewick's Swan. Like other swans, seen on lakes, rivers, estuaries and sheltered water on coast. Most winter in Scotland and northern England, migrating from Iceland. 152 cm.

Yellow area comes to a point towards tip of beak

Upper neck straight, lower part near body often bent

Geese

Has short pink bill with black on base and tip

Pink legs

◀ Pink-footed Goose

Smaller, greyer bird than Bean Goose. Head and neck appear very dark at a distance. Winters in Scotland and northern England. 68 cm.

Bean Goose ▶

Larger and rarer than Pink-footed Goose. A winter visitor, seen grazing inland in western Scotland and East Anglia. 80 cm.

Heavy bill

Orange and black bill

Orange legs

◀ Greylag Goose

Seen in winter mainly in Scotland. A few stay to breed in the Hebrides. Elsewhere, reintroduced birds seen all year on lakes, reservoirs, gravel pits. 82 cm.

Geese

Lesser
White-fronted Goose ▶

Very rare but regular
winter visitor. Usually in
flocks with European
White-fronted Goose. It
feeds at a more
rapid rate than
European. 60 cm.

More white on crown
than European
White-fronted Goose

Pink
bill

Yellow eye ring

Orange
legs

European race
has pink bill
and orange legs

◀ European
White-fronted Goose

Winter migrant from
Russia. Largest flocks
winter on Severn estuary.
All the adult White-fronted
geese have
barring on
belly. 71 cm.

European and Greenland
White-fronted Geese are
different races of the
same species

Greenland
White-fronted Goose ▶

Winters in Ireland,
western Scotland and a few
in Wales. A darker bird
than European, with
heavier belly
markings.
72 cm.

Greenland race has orange
bill and orange legs

Geese

Snow Goose ▶

A rare visitor from
North America. Has two
different colour phases –
white and blue. Usually
seen amongst flock of
other "grey" geese such as
Greylag or
Pink-footed
Geese. 68 cm.

Blue phase

White phase

Red-breasted
is the smallest
of all geese

Very small
short bill

◀ Red-breasted Goose

Very rare winter visitor.
Breeds in the Russian
Arctic. When seen it is
usually with White-fronted
or Brent Geese. Seen
occasionally as an
escape from
wildfowl
collections. 54 cm.

More white on
head than
Canada Goose

Barnacle Goose ▶

Two wintering populations
in Britain. One in Ireland
and Islay, which breeds in
Greenland. The other,
which breeds north of
Norway, winters
on Solway
Firth. 63 cm.

Geese

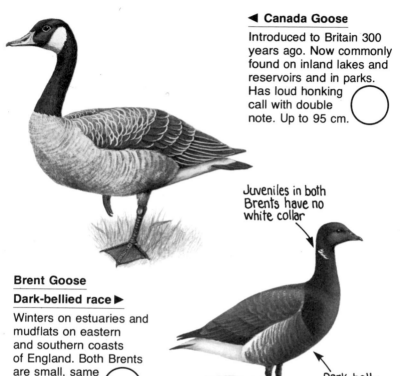

◄ Canada Goose

Introduced to Britain 300 years ago. Now commonly found on inland lakes and reservoirs and in parks. Has loud honking call with double note. Up to 95 cm.

Juveniles in both Brents have no white collar

Dark belly

Brent Goose
Dark-bellied race ►

Winters on estuaries and mudflats on eastern and southern coasts of England. Both Brents are small, same size as a Mallard. 58 cm.

Light belly

Seen feeding on eel grass on mudflats

◄ Brent Goose
Light-bellied race

One population winters in Lindisfarne, Northumbria, breeding in Spitzbergen, north of Norway. Another winters in Ireland, breeding in Greenland. 58 cm.

Estuary ducks

♀ has no knob on bill but has white feathers at its base

♀

♂

◀ Shelduck

Found on coasts and estuaries, often in flocks. Feeds on small molluscs in very shallow water. Nests in rabbit holes, often on sand dunes. 61 cm.

Wigeon ▶

The only duck which grazes regularly. Forms large flocks near coasts and on the Ouse Washes, Norfolk. Also on lakes and reservoirs. 46 cm.

Drake has bright yellow forehead

♀

♂

Wigeon are often seen grazing on fields near water

American Wigeon ▶

Rare visitor, mostly occurring in Ireland in winter. Greyer and less colourful than Wigeon. Forehead in male cream rather than yellow. 47 cm.

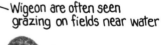

♀

♂

Diving ducks

♀ Scaup has no tuft on head

♂

◄ Scaup

Winter visitor to bays and estuaries. Similar to Tufted Duck but look for grey back on drake, and more white at base of bill in female. 48 cm.

Tuft

♀

♂

Tufted Duck ►

Commonest black and white diving duck. Both a winter visitor and a resident breeder. Seen on large lakes and reservoirs. 43 cm.

Peak on head

♀

♂

◄ Ring-necked Duck

Rare visitor from North America. Very similar to Tufted Duck but has peak not tuft on top of head. Duck has white eye ring and white near bill. 43 cm.

Goldeneye ►

Mainly seen in winter on freshwater and on coast. A few breed in Scotland. Nests in tree holes. White wing bars show in flight. 46 cm.

♀

♂

Diving ducks

♂ ♀

Pochard drake is distinguished from Wigeon by pure chestnut head and neck and black breast

◀ Pochard

Seen on lowland fresh-water lakes and reservoirs. Dives to feed on water plants. Often seen with other kinds of diving duck. 46 cm.

Red-crested Pochard ▶

Rare visitor from southern Europe. Seen mostly in eastern England. In flight its white hindwing shows. 55 cm.

Duck has pale cheek

♀

♂

Drake has red bill and red legs

♀

♂

White under tail

◀ Ferruginous Duck

Occasionally seen in Britain, mainly in winter. Breeds in southern and eastern Europe. Usually with other diving ducks, on freshwater. 40 cm.

Sawbills

Crest in both duck and drake

♀

♂

◀ **Red-breasted**

Red-breasted

Merganser

Breeds Scotland, Ireland and northern England in dense cover alongside freshwater. In winter seen on estuaries and coasts. 58 cm.

♀

Crest shows only in female

♂

Goosander ▶

Breeds in Scotland. Nests in tree holes. Favours fast-flowing streams and rivers in summer, and lakes and reservoirs in winter. 66 cm.

Sawbills are diving ducks. They have saw-edged bills for gripping live fish.

Smew ▶

Occasional winter visitor to reservoirs and estuaries. Breeds by freshwater in forests in north Europe. Males seen more in Britain than females. 41 cm.

♀

♂

Sea ducks

Duck is pale over much of head

♀

♂

Drake is the only all-black duck

Has black feet

◀ Common Scoter

A few breed in northern Scotland. Mainly seen during winter on coastal water, especially in south and east England. Often in flocks. 46 cm.

Velvet Scoter ▶

Seen mainly as winter visitor on coastal water. Often with Common Scoters or Eiders. Look for its white secondary feathers in flight. 56 cm.

Two pale patches on head

♀

♂

White "tear" round eye

Has red feet

♀

♂

Large multi-coloured bill

◀ Surf Scoter

Regular but rare visitor from North America to coastal waters. No white wing bar in flight. Female very similar to Velvet with extra nape patch. 50 cm.

Sea ducks

Eider ▶

Breeds near seashores in northern Britain and in northern Europe.
Seen in winter further south off rocky or sandy coasts. The soft down taken from its nest after young are hatched is used for stuffing eiderdowns. 58 cm.

♂ ♀

See page 49 for illustration of immature and eclipse plumage of Eider drake

◀ King Eider

Very rare winter visitor. Breeds in the Arctic. Drake unmistakable, with huge orange forehead. Female usually a redder brown than Eider duck. 56 cm.

♀

♂

Both sexes have more black on head in summer

♀ Winter

Long-tailed Duck ▶

Breeds in the Arctic and also on some mountains in Scandinavia.
Winters in some numbers round British coasts, very occasionally on inland reservoirs.
Drake 53 cm.
Duck 41 cm.

♂ Winter

Dabbling ducks

Mallard

The most widespread of all wildfowl, found on all kinds of still and slow-moving water. In winter also on estuaries. Many live all year in Britain, but numbers are increased by migrants from the continent each autumn. Most kinds of domestic duck are descended from Mallard. Wild Mallard often cross-breed with domestic ducks. 58 cm.

▲ Just before the breeding season, "pursuit flights" are often seen. Two or more drakes chase one female. Courtship continues on water.

Mallard drake in "eclipse plumage" – ▼ during its moult. In most European species of duck, drakes are seen in eclipse plumage for several weeks in summer after the breeding period. See also page 54.

♂

It looks similar to ♀ but look for olive-green bill

◀ Mallard ducklings, like all wildfowl young, hatch out with eyes open. They are soon able to leave the nest and feed themselves.

Covered in downy feathers

♀

Blue speculum

♂

Dabbling ducks

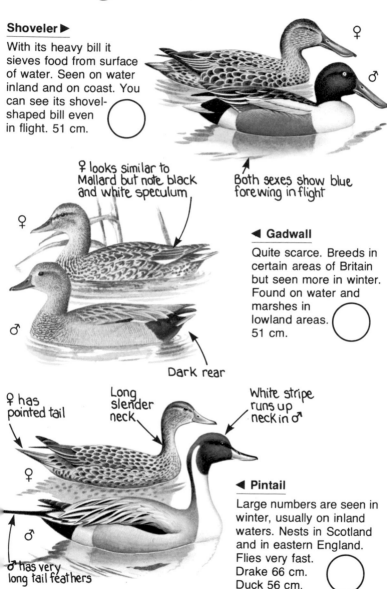

Shoveler ▶

With its heavy bill it sieves food from surface of water. Seen on water inland and on coast. You can see its shovel-shaped bill even in flight. 51 cm.

♀

♂

♀ looks similar to Mallard but note black and white speculum

Both sexes show blue forewing in flight

♀

♂

Dark rear

◀ Gadwall

Quite scarce. Breeds in certain areas of Britain but seen more in winter. Found on water and marshes in lowland areas. 51 cm.

♀ has pointed tail

Long slender neck

White stripe runs up neck in ♂

♀

♂

♂ has very long tail feathers

◀ Pintail

Large numbers are seen in winter, usually on inland waters. Nests in Scotland and in eastern England. Flies very fast.
Drake 66 cm.
Duck 56 cm.

19

Dabbling ducks

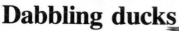

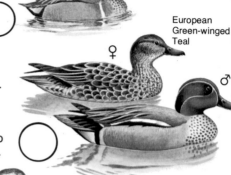

American Green-winged Teal

European Green-winged Teal

American Green-winged Teal ▶

A rare visitor. Has white stripe on side of breast. Both species small: 35 cm.

European Green-winged Teal ▶

Breeds by freshwater. Also on coastal water in winter.

◀ Garganey

A summer visitor, breeding mainly in eastern England. Nests near shallow water. Winters in Africa. Note white stripe over eye in drake. 38 cm.

Blue-winged Teal ▶

Rare but regular visitor from North America. The pale blue on its wings shows in flight. 38 cm.

◀ Marbled Teal

One of the rarest ducks to breed in Europe. Seen in summer in southern Spain and France. Male and female are alike. 41 cm.

Perching ducks, stifftails

Mandarin Duck ▶

Introduced from China. Several small wild populations now found in Britain, especially in the south. Nests in tree holes. 46 cm.

♀

♂

♀

♂

◀ Carolina Duck

Introduced from North America. Seen also as an escape from waterfowl collections. Nests in holes and perches in trees, like Mandarin. 48 cm.

Ruddy Duck ▶

Originally from North America. Now lives wild on a number of reservoirs in Avon, S.W. Midlands and Cheshire. In courtship display male beats chest and makes bubbles. 39 cm.

♀

♂

Stiff tails are sometimes seen with tails sticking up. Their long, stiff tail feathers help direct them when diving

♀

♂

◀ White-headed Duck

The European counterpart of Ruddy Duck. Extremely rare in Britain. Now a rare breeding bird in southern Europe. 45 cm.

Rails

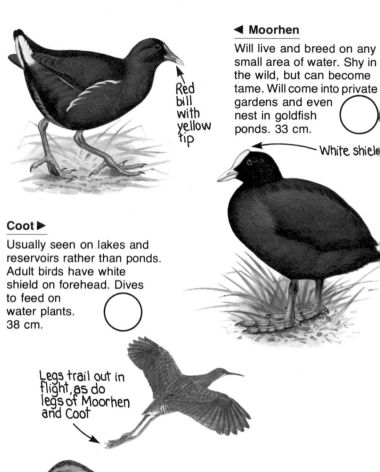

Red bill with yellow tip

◀ Moorhen

Will live and breed on any small area of water. Shy in the wild, but can become tame. Will come into private gardens and even nest in goldfish ponds. 33 cm.

White shield

Coot ▶

Usually seen on lakes and reservoirs rather than ponds. Adult birds have white shield on forehead. Dives to feed on water plants. 38 cm.

Legs trail out in flight, as do legs of Moorhen and Coot

Barring

◀ Water Rail

Lives in wetlands especially reed beds. A secretive bird. Listen for its piglet-like squeal and grunting noises. Swims for short distances. 28 cm.

Divers, grebe

Red-throated Diver ▶

Breeds in the Scottish highlands near freshwater. Winters at sea. The most commonly seen diver. In winter note head – whiter than other divers. 56 cm.

Winter

Summer

Winter

Summer

◀ Black-throated Diver

Breeds in the Scottish Highlands near large areas of freshwater. Winters at sea. Grey on head in winter plumage. Call is a loud wailing cry. 60 cm.

Great Northern Diver ▶

Rarely breeds in Britain. Seen in winter on coasts. Black on head in winter. Like all divers, swims well and dives from surface of water for food. 75 cm.

Summer

Winter

Crest expands during display

Summer

Winter

◀ Great Crested Grebe

Found on lakes, reservoirs, flooded gravel pits. Also on coast in winter. Breeds in many areas of Britain. Beautiful court-ship display in spring. 48 cm.

23

Grebes

Winter

Chestnut cheeks and throat

Summer

◄ Little Grebe or Dabchick

Seen on slow-moving water with thick vegetation at edges. A secretive bird. Its call is a shrill trill. 27 cm.

Slavonian Grebe ►

Regular winter visitor on coasts. A few breed in Scotland. In winter looks similar to Black-necked Grebe but note crown and straight bill. 33 cm.

Winter

Summer

Summer

Winter

Black and yellow bill

◄ Red-necked Grebe

Winter visitor to Britain. Seen on coastal water. In winter looks similar to Great Crested Grebe but look for black and yellow bill, and also crown. 43 cm.

Black-necked Grebe ►

Common winter visitor. Breeds in a few places in Britain. In winter similar to Slavonian but note deeper crown and upturned bill. 30 cm.

Winter

Summer

Upturned bill

Spoonbill, flamingo

Spoonbill ▶

Rare but regular visitor to Britain, mainly to east and south-west England. Favours shallow water, fresh and coastal. Breeds in southern Europe. 86 cm.

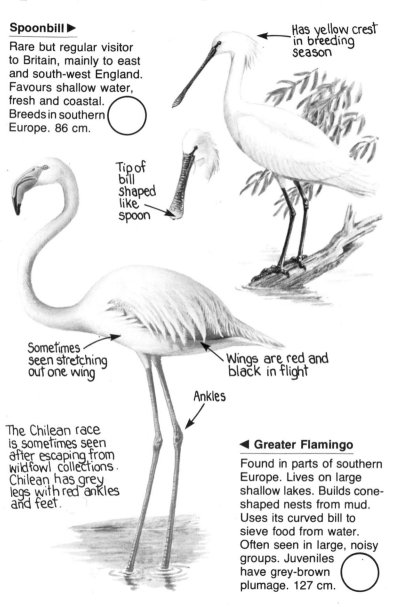

Has yellow crest in breeding season

Tip of bill shaped like spoon

Sometimes seen stretching out one wing

Wings are red and black in flight

Ankles

The Chilean race is sometimes seen after escaping from wildfowl collections. Chilean has grey legs with red ankles and feet.

◀ Greater Flamingo

Found in parts of southern Europe. Lives on large shallow lakes. Builds cone-shaped nests from mud. Uses its curved bill to sieve food from water. Often seen in large, noisy groups. Juveniles have grey-brown plumage. 127 cm.

Storks

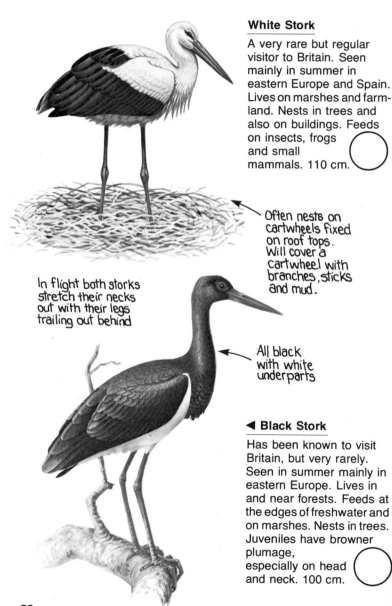

White Stork

A very rare but regular visitor to Britain. Seen mainly in summer in eastern Europe and Spain. Lives on marshes and farmland. Nests in trees and also on buildings. Feeds on insects, frogs and small mammals. 110 cm.

Often nests on cartwheels fixed on roof tops. Will cover a cartwheel with branches, sticks and mud.

In flight both storks stretch their necks out with their legs trailing out behind

All black with white underparts

◀ Black Stork

Has been known to visit Britain, but very rarely. Seen in summer mainly in eastern Europe. Lives in and near forests. Feeds at the edges of freshwater and on marshes. Nests in trees. Juveniles have browner plumage, especially on head and neck. 100 cm.

Crane, heron

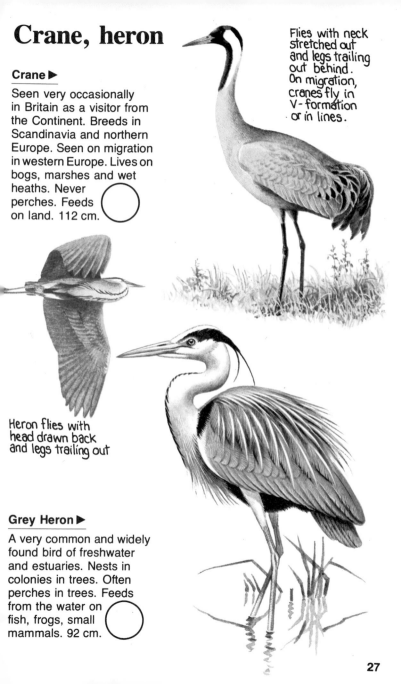

Flies with neck stretched out and legs trailing out behind. On migration, cranes fly in V-formation or in lines.

Crane ▶

Seen very occasionally in Britain as a visitor from the Continent. Breeds in Scandinavia and northern Europe. Seen on migration in western Europe. Lives on bogs, marshes and wet heaths. Never perches. Feeds on land. 112 cm.

Heron flies with head drawn back and legs trailing out

Grey Heron ▶

A very common and widely found bird of freshwater and estuaries. Nests in colonies in trees. Often perches in trees. Feeds from the water on fish, frogs, small mammals. 92 cm.

Herons, bittern

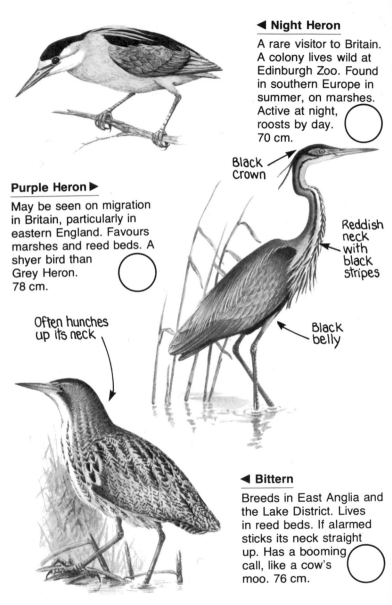

◀ Night Heron

A rare visitor to Britain. A colony lives wild at Edinburgh Zoo. Found in southern Europe in summer, on marshes. Active at night, roosts by day. 70 cm.

Black Crown

Purple Heron ▶

May be seen on migration in Britain, particularly in eastern England. Favours marshes and reed beds. A shyer bird than Grey Heron. 78 cm.

Reddish neck with black stripes

Often hunches up its neck

Black belly

◀ Bittern

Breeds in East Anglia and the Lake District. Lives in reed beds. If alarmed sticks its neck straight up. Has a booming call, like a cow's moo. 76 cm.

Egrets

Little Egret ▶

Appears annually in Britain on passage, on marshes and near shallow water. Like all herons and egrets, flies with bent neck and with legs straight. 55 cm.

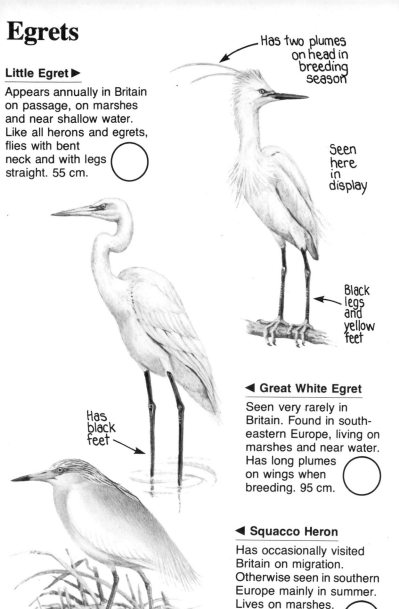

Has two plumes on head in breeding season

Seen here in display

Black legs and yellow feet

Has black feet

◀ Great White Egret

Seen very rarely in Britain. Found in south-eastern Europe, living on marshes and near water. Has long plumes on wings when breeding. 95 cm.

◀ Squacco Heron

Has occasionally visited Britain on migration. Otherwise seen in southern Europe mainly in summer. Lives on marshes. Nests in trees. 45 cm.

Kingfisher, wagtail, dipper

Kingfisher ▶

Brilliantly coloured. Seen
near lakes and rivers.
Usually perches near water
before diving for fish.
Has a shrill
piping call
in flight. 16 cm.

Usually flies
low and
straight
over
water

Often seen wagging its
very long tail up and down

♂
Summer

Blue-grey
on top

◀ Grey Wagtail

Seen near freshwater,
especially fast-flowing
streams. Catches insects
in flight over water. Male
has black bib
in summer.
18 cm.

Northern Europe

Has no
reddish-
brown
underparts

Britain and
Central Europe

Dipper ▶

Swims and dives well. Can
walk along bottom of fast-
flowing streams. Also seen
flying low and fast over
the water. Breeds
in north and west
Britain. 18 cm.

Reddish-
brown
underneath

Bunting, warblers, harrier

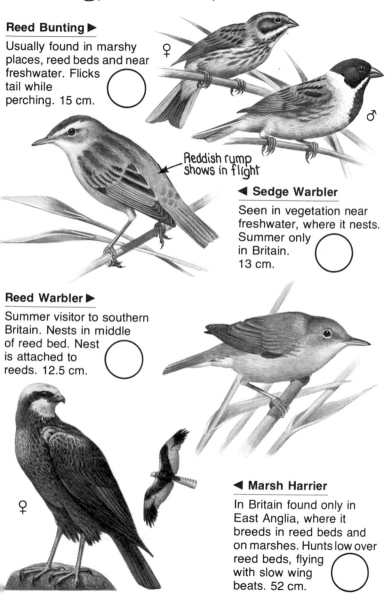

Reed Bunting ▶

Usually found in marshy places, reed beds and near freshwater. Flicks tail while perching. 15 cm.

Reddish rump shows in flight

◀ Sedge Warbler

Seen in vegetation near freshwater, where it nests. Summer only in Britain. 13 cm.

Reed Warbler ▶

Summer visitor to southern Britain. Nests in middle of reed bed. Nest is attached to reeds. 12.5 cm.

◀ Marsh Harrier

In Britain found only in East Anglia, where it breeds in reed beds and on marshes. Hunts low over reed beds, flying with slow wing beats. 52 cm.

Birds of prey

Osprey ▶

Rare summer visitor to Britain. Breeding pairs nest in Scotland. Single birds may be seen in other parts with large areas of water and fish. 56 cm.

Strong claws for gripping slippery fish

Varies from dark to light grey on top

Black streak on cheek like a moustache

◀ Peregrine

Seen on estuaries and coastal marshes in winter. Breeds on cliffs as well as mountain crags. On coast will feed on sea birds, waders or ducks. 39–50 cm.

Has very broad wings

White-tailed Sea Eagle ▶

Became extinct in Britain in the last century. It is being reintroduced on Rhum, on west coast of Scotland. Feeds on fish and sea birds. 68–97 cm.

Short white tail

Gulls

Black-headed Gull ▶

Very common gull. Seen as often inland as on coast. Nests in colonies on marshes, dunes, shingle. Head is dark in summer only. 38 cm.

Winter

Pale edge to wing

Summer

◀ Lesser Black-backed Gull

Mainly a summer visitor, though some winter in Britain. Similar to Herring Gull but look out for its much darker grey back. 55 cm.

Orange-yellow legs

Greater Black-backed Gull ▶

Britain's largest gull. Not often seen inland. Nests on rocky coasts. Usually seen in ones or twos. Back is blacker than Lesser Black-backed Gull's. 70 cm.

Pinkish legs

Gulls

◀ Herring Gull

A common, noisy gull seen on coasts and inland. Scavenges food from people and off rubbish dumps. Will drop shellfish from a height to open. 62 cm.

Common Gull ▶

Can be confused with Kittiwake but look for colour of legs. In summer on coasts and near fresh-water inland. In winter also on farmland. 40 cm.

◀ Kittiwake

Nests in colonies on cliffs. When not breeding spends most time well out at sea. Often seen following ships. Note black legs. 43 cm.

Terns

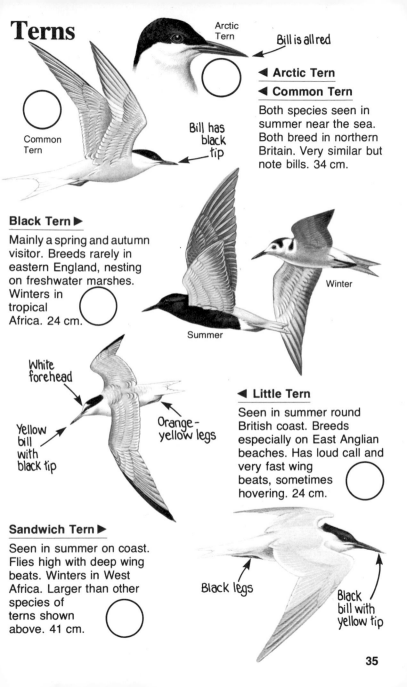

Arctic Tern

Bill is all red

◄ Arctic Tern

◄ Common Tern

Both species seen in summer near the sea. Both breed in northern Britain. Very similar but note bills. 34 cm.

Common Tern

Bill has black tip

Black Tern ►

Mainly a spring and autumn visitor. Breeds rarely in eastern England, nesting on freshwater marshes. Winters in tropical Africa. 24 cm.

Winter

Summer

White forehead

Yellow bill with black tip

Orange-yellow legs

◄ Little Tern

Seen in summer round British coast. Breeds especially on East Anglian beaches. Has loud call and very fast wing beats, sometimes hovering. 24 cm.

Sandwich Tern ►

Seen in summer on coast. Flies high with deep wing beats. Winters in West Africa. Larger than other species of terns shown above. 41 cm.

Black legs

Black bill with yellow tip

35

Skuas, fulmar

Great Skua ▶

A large, heavy-looking bird, seen out at sea. A few breed in northern Scotland on moorland. Like all skuas, chases other sea birds to rob them of their food. 58 cm.

White patch on top of wing and underneath

In dark phase (not shown) is brown all over

Pale phase

◀ Arctic Skua

Seen out at sea, also breeding in northern Scotland. Same size as a Black-headed Gull. Has two colour phases, dark and pale. 50 cm.

Fulmar ▶

Seen out at sea except during breeding season. Nests in colonies on sea cliffs all round Britain. Looks rather similar to gull, but note straight gliding flight on stiff wings with short wing beats. 47 cm.

Looks rather like Herring Gull but has no black wing tips

Sits, never stands on land

Shearwater, petrels

All dark above, white underneath

◀ Manx Shearwater

Seen out at sea. Lands only to breed. Nests in colonies on islands, in holes or rabbit burrows, visiting at night so not attacked by gulls. 35 cm.

May be seen in flocks at dusk, waiting to land at breeding ground

Storm Petrel ▶

Seen at sea flying low over water. Follows ships. Smallest European sea bird, same size as a House Sparrow. Breeds on rocky islands in Scotland and Ireland. 15 cm.

Pale patch on underwing

White rump

Dark underwing

Forked tail difficult to see in flight

◀ Leach's Petrel

Looks similar to Storm Petrel but note dark underwing. Has zig-zag flight. Does not follow ships. Mostly seen in winter out at sea. 20 cm.

Auks

Neck and throat are white in winter

◄ Razorbill

Nests in colonies on cliffs and rocky shores. Winters at sea. Dives for fish. Its flat-sided bill makes it easy to distinguish from other auks. 41 cm.

Neck and throat are white in winter

Guillemot ►

The most commonly seen auk. Nests on cliff ledges in large, noisy groups. Some northern birds have a white eye ring and white line on their heads. 42 cm.

Summer

Black Guillemot ►

Black in summer, with white wing patch. In winter turns white on lower parts with barred black and white on top. Note bright red legs. 35 cm.

Summer

Brightly coloured bill in summer

◄ Puffin

Lives far out at sea except in breeding season. Nests in colonies in burrows on turfy cliff tops and islands. A very small auk. 30 cm.

Summer

Cormorants, gannet

◀ Shag

Seen on rocky coasts.
Nests in colonies. Like
Cormorant, dives for fish.
Crest is seen only in the
breeding season.
Young are
brown. 76 cm.

◀ Gannet

Seen out at sea except
when nesting on rocky
coasts. Dives headfirst
into the sea from a
height to catch
fish. Young are
browner. 91 cm.

Cormorant ▼

Seen mostly near the sea
but also inland on lakes and
reservoirs. Nests in
colonies on
rocky ledges.
90 cm.

Often
perches and
stretches wings
to dry in the sun

Has white
patch in
breeding season

Waders

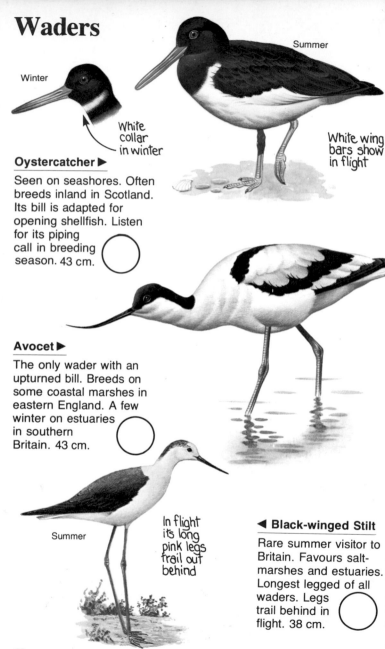

Winter

Summer

White collar in winter

Oystercatcher ▶

Seen on seashores. Often breeds inland in Scotland. Its bill is adapted for opening shellfish. Listen for its piping call in breeding season. 43 cm.

White wing bars show in flight

Avocet ▶

The only wader with an upturned bill. Breeds on some coastal marshes in eastern England. A few winter on estuaries in southern Britain. 43 cm.

Summer

In flight its long pink legs trail out behind

◀ Black-winged Stilt

Rare summer visitor to Britain. Favours salt-marshes and estuaries. Longest legged of all waders. Legs trail behind in flight. 38 cm.

Waders

Juvenile

Broad white bar on wing →

Summer

◀ Ringed Plover

Seen on sandy and shingle shores, also estuaries in winter. Usually nests on shingle bars on coast or more rarely inland. 19 cm.

Wing bar rarely shows in flight

Summer

◀ Little Ringed Plover.

Summer visitor. Gravel pits and shingle banks inland near freshwater. Has less black on forehead than Ringed Plover, and thinner, blacker beak. Also has yellow eye ring. 15 cm.

Kentish Plover ▶

Summer visitor to southern England. Seen on sand or shingle, usually on coast. Slimmer than the Ringed Plovers, with longer, blacker legs. 16 cm.

Reddish-brown on crown

Black band does not form a complete ring

♂

Black legs

Waders

Golden Plover ▶

Forms large flocks outside the breeding season, often with Lapwings. Some breed on moors. Winters inland as well as on estuaries and muddy shores. 28 cm.

Northern Europe

Southern Europe

Winter

Grey Plover ▶

Winter visitor. Especially seen on eastern and southern coasts of Britain. Seen in small groups, mixed with other waders. 28 cm.

Summer

Winter

Summer

Winter

◀ Turnstone

Moves along shore uncovering food from under stones. Seen on shingle or rocky shores. Does not nest in Britain, but may be seen most months of the year. 23 cm.

Waders

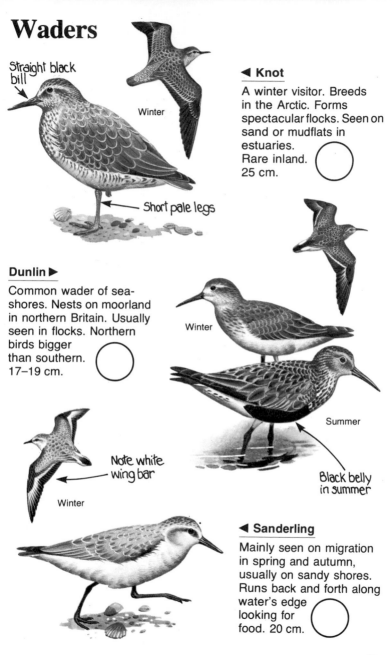

Straight black bill

Winter

Short pale legs

◀ Knot

A winter visitor. Breeds in the Arctic. Forms spectacular flocks. Seen on sand or mudflats in estuaries. Rare inland. 25 cm.

Dunlin ▶

Common wader of sea-shores. Nests on moorland in northern Britain. Usually seen in flocks. Northern birds bigger than southern. 17–19 cm.

Winter

Summer

Note white wing bar

Winter

Black belly in summer

◀ Sanderling

Mainly seen on migration in spring and autumn, usually on sandy shores. Runs back and forth along water's edge looking for food. 20 cm.

Waders

Lapwing ▶

Present all year. Forms large flocks in winter on farmland, estuaries and mudflats. The most commonly seen wader in much of Europe. 30 cm.

Broad rounded wings

Crest

◀ Common Sandpiper

Nests by upland streams and lakes. Winters near freshwater. Often seen perching and bobbing its head and tail. 20 cm.

Purple gloss on back hardly shows

Summer

Purple Sandpiper ▶

Winter visitor. Also seen on passage in spring and autumn. Seen mainly on rocky shores. Purple gloss on back barely visible. 21 cm.

Winter

44

Waders

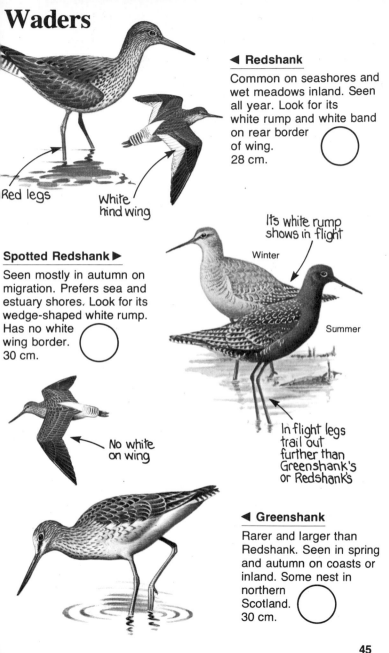

◄ Redshank

Common on seashores and wet meadows inland. Seen all year. Look for its white rump and white band on rear border of wing. 28 cm.

Red legs

White hind wing

Spotted Redshank ►

Seen mostly in autumn on migration. Prefers sea and estuary shores. Look for its wedge-shaped white rump. Has no white wing border. 30 cm.

No white on wing

Its white rump shows in flight

Winter

Summer

In flight legs trail out further than Greenshank's or Redshank's

◄ Greenshank

Rarer and larger than Redshank. Seen in spring and autumn on coasts or inland. Some nest in northern Scotland. 30 cm.

Waders

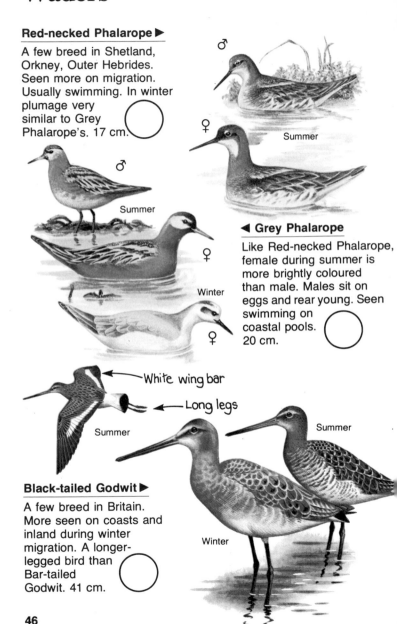

Red-necked Phalarope ▶

A few breed in Shetland, Orkney, Outer Hebrides. Seen more on migration. Usually swimming. In winter plumage very similar to Grey Phalarope's. 17 cm.

♂ Summer

♀ Summer

♂ Summer

♀ Winter

◀ Grey Phalarope

Like Red-necked Phalarope, female during summer is more brightly coloured than male. Males sit on eggs and rear young. Seen swimming on coastal pools. 20 cm.

White wing bar

Long legs

Summer

Summer

Black-tailed Godwit ▶

A few breed in Britain. More seen on coasts and inland during winter migration. A longer-legged bird than Bar-tailed Godwit. 41 cm.

Winter

Waders

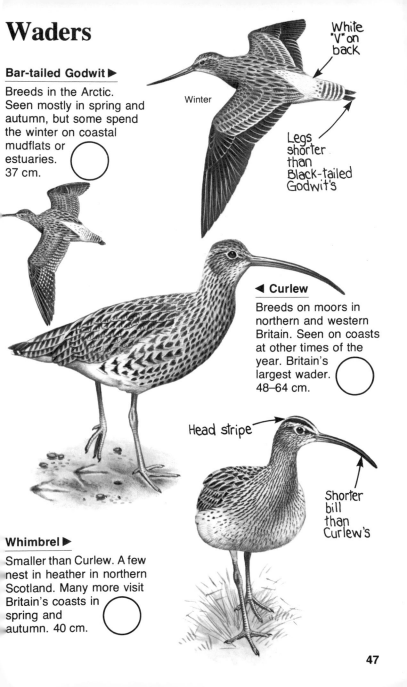

Bar-tailed Godwit ▶

Breeds in the Arctic.
Seen mostly in spring and
autumn, but some spend
the winter on coastal
mudflats or
estuaries.
37 cm.

White
"V" on
back

Winter

Legs
shorter
than
Black-tailed
Godwit's

◀ Curlew

Breeds on moors in
northern and western
Britain. Seen on coasts
at other times of the
year. Britain's
largest wader.
48–64 cm.

Head stripe

Shorter
bill
than
Curlew's

Whimbrel ▶

Smaller than Curlew. A few
nest in heather in northern
Scotland. Many more visit
Britain's coasts in
spring and
autumn. 40 cm.

Waders

◀ Ruff

Seen mainly in spring and autumn, some also winter in wet places. Male's summer plumage with ruff and ear tufts varies in colour.
Female 23 cm.
Male 29 cm.

♂ Summer   Winter ♂

Woodcock ▶

Secretive bird of moist woodlands. Feeds usually at night on marshy ground. Watch out for its display flight over woods at dusk in early summer. 34 cm.

Snipe →

Woodc

◀ Snipe

Breeds in marshes and we meadows. In winter seen near freshwater. Zigzag flight and harsh call when disturbed. Well camouflaged. 27 cm.

48

Changing plumages

Eclipse plumage
In all European species of duck except the Shelduck, the drakes are seen in a duller plumage during their moult. This is called the eclipse plumage (see also the Mallard on page 18). You will need a special reference book to identify drakes in eclipse plumage.

Juvenile and immature plumages
Some birds take several years to reach adult plumage. For instance the Eider drake may be three years old before it reaches full breeding plumage.

Gulls may also take up to three years, going through different stages before showing adult plumage. Some species of gulls are difficult to distinguish from one another in their juvenile stages. You will need a reference book to identify gulls at these stages.

Eider

♂ adult breeding

♂
2nd year immature breeding

♂ adult eclipse

Black-headed Gull

Juvenile

1st winter

Adult (winter)

Changes from season to season
Many waders seen in Britain in the autumn and spring are passing through (they are called passage migrants). They are on their way to, or from, breeding grounds further north or wintering grounds further south. So their plumages are very often halfway between summer and winter. Some species, however, like Lapwing, show little change from season to season.

Moulting, changing over from winter to summer plumage

Sanderling

Winter

Summer

Bodies, wings, feet and beaks

Body Shapes

▼Dabbling ducks have their legs placed at the centre of the body. They appear to walk more comfortably on land than diving ducks.

▼Diving ducks have their legs positioned to the rear of the body where they act as a propeller when diving; they walk clumsily on land.

Divers, auks and cormorants are separate families of birds which dive for fish. They have all developed legs positioned to the rear of the body where they can more easily propel the bird under water.

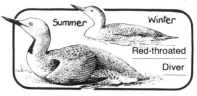

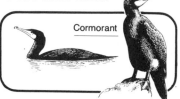

▲Divers' legs are positioned so far back for underwater swimming that they slide on their bellies rather than walk on land.

▲Cormorants and auks have legs positioned so far back that their bodies are upright when standing.

Wing shapes

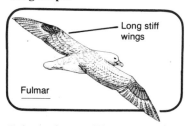

Fulmars have stiff, narrow wings shaped to enable them to glide for long periods over the sea on winds.

Auks have small wings which they can use both for flight and for 'paddle flying' under water.

Feet

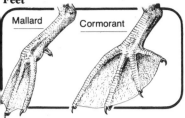

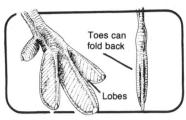

▲Wildfowl, divers, auks and cormorants have webs between their toes to act as paddles when swimming through or under water.

▲Grebes have "lobes" round their toes for swimming and diving. They fold back on the forward stroke and open out on the back stroke.

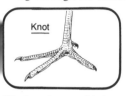

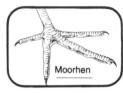

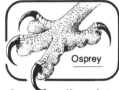

Waders have widely-spread toes for walking on mud and sand. Some species, e.g. Avocet, have partly webbed toes to help them swim.

Moorhens have very long toes. The toe-pads expand under pressure to give a wider area on which to walk across mud or water vegetation.

Ospreys dive into water to catch fish with their feet. Their huge claws and the spiny scales underneath their feet help to grasp slippery fish.

Beaks

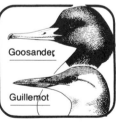

Barnacle Geese have shorter bills than most geese, since they feed on short vegetation, usually on saltwater marshes.

Goosander and Guillemot are both fish feeders. Though each is from a different family, (Goosander a duck, Guillemot an auk) the shape of their beaks is similar.

Flamingos feed by filtering tiny animals and plant life from the water. The fine "serrations" edging their bill help to sieve food from the water.

Feeding

Sea Birds

Sea ducks like the Eider find food on the sea bed in shallow water

Cormorants dive after fish using their feet to propel them

Auks like the Razorbill dive for fish using their wings and feet to propel them

Phalaropes seize food from the surface of the sea

Waders

Estuary mud is very rich in food for waders. Each species of wader has a different shaped beak, varying from short and stubby to long and curved. With these they are able to find food at different depths in the mud.

Turnstone uses beak to look under pebbles for small animal life

Ringed Plovers seek small snails (hydrobia) on the mud surface

Knot (*left*) and Redshank (*right*) "probe" the mud with their bills for types of shrimps and ragworms

Wildfowl

Greylag Geese have heavy bills for breaking into soft ground for roots

Teal dabble for seeds at water's edge

Barnacle Geese graze on short grasses on saltmarshes

Wigeon are the only duck species to graze regularly

Gannets and terns plunge headfirst into the water from flight

Skuas chase other sea birds like terns to make them drop their fish

Gulls skim over the water taking food from the surface

The Bar-tailed Godwit (*left*) and Curlew (*right*) can "probe" quite deep into the mud for lugworms, ragworms and deeper-living shellfish

Oystercatchers open up cockles and other shellfish

Bewick's Swans reach into deeper water for underwater weeds

Shoveler sieves seeds and small animals from the water surface

Mallard (*left*) and Pintail (*right*) "upend" for seeds, underwater plants and small animal life at different depths

Pochard feed mainly on plant food in deeper water. They dive to reach it.

Migration

Birds migrate not so much to escape the cold but to follow available food supplies.

A large number migrate north in spring towards or into the *arctic circle* in order to breed. A few examples of birds which do this are Bewick's and Whooper Swans, White-fronted and Pink-footed Geese, some terns and many waders. They do this because the arctic has these advantages:

1) The short arctic summer produces a rich variety of body-building foods for fast-growing young birds. For example there is a good supply of vegetation for young geese (goslings) and many insects, such as mosquito larvae, for ducklings and wader chicks.

2) During the short arctic summer it stays light all day and night, so the birds have more daylight hours in which to feed.

3) There are fewer predators in the arctic, and less disturbance from people. This makes nesting and rearing young birds easier.

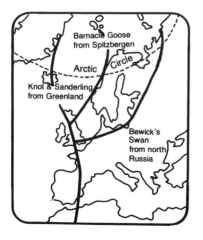

A large number of birds migrate *further south* to winter in milder climates where more food is available. For example, the White Stork migrates from its breeding ground in central Europe to winter in southern Africa, where it finds insects like locusts and small mammals and frogs, which are not available in a European winter.

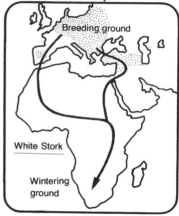

The *British Isles*, including Eire, is a wintering place for birds, especially wildfowl. It is also a stopping off place for birds on passage, mainly terns and waders which are migrating further south.

Britain is a particularly good wintering ground because of its winters which are quite mild in comparison with those of other European countries. The mild winters are due to the influence of the Gulf Stream bathing the British Isles with relatively warm water. Therefore the shorelines, estuaries and freshwater wetlands rarely freeze, so birds can easily forage for food all winter.

Things to collect

Feathers

On your bird spotting adventures you may come across moulted feathers. Try and work out which species or group of birds (e.g. gulls) they belong to. Is it a body, tail or wing feather? If from the wing, is it a primary or secondary flight feather?

Feathers can be sellotaped onto paper and labelled with notes of where and when they were found. You can keep the pages in a loose-leaf file or in a photograph album with clear plastic sleeves.

Skulls

You may find skulls already "cleaned" by organisms and bleached by the sun. If you find a corpse, you can bury it to let the flesh decompose naturally. After six months, dig it up and take the skull. Always wash your hands after handling corpses and bones.

Mallard

Pellets

Herons, gulls and waders all cough up pellets formed from the undigested remains of food. Look for pellets at roosting and feeding places. You can examine these and work out what the bird has eaten. You can also preserve them by dipping them into liquid varnish.

This pellet contains vole fur

Bones

A heron pellet. These usually consist of fur rather than fish bones and scales. This is because the heron is able to digest all parts of a fish.

Look for gull pellets in places where they have been feeding. They are usually very loose pellets and contain things like fish bones and the remains of plants.

Recording footprints

Try making plaster casts of clear footprints, for instance of ducks, herons or moorhens.

Surround the footprint with a piece of card about 30 cm long and 5 cm wide. Mix water with the plaster of paris until it feels like thin porridge. Pour in the plaster to the depth of 2–3 cm. Let it dry for at least 15 minutes, and clean it up when you get home.

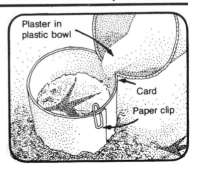

Plaster in plastic bowl

Card

Paper clip

The Wildfowl Trust

This symbol of the Wildfowl Trust shows two Bewick's Swans, the smallest and rarest of the three European swan species.

The Trust is concerned with the conservation of wildfowl and wetland habitats. These Bewick's Swans symbolise a story which reflects the birds' confidence in the Trust's conservation efforts.

It started in 1946 when Sir Peter Scott founded the Wildfowl Trust at Slimbridge on the River Severn in Gloucestershire. The Severn Estuary and in particular the Slimbridge saltmarshes had been known as an important wintering area for many species of wildfowl for centuries. But there was no record of any Bewick's Swans ever having visited it.

In 1948 a wild Bewick's Swan flew into the ground, joined some North American Whistling Swans in the Trust's collection of wildfowl, and then stayed for the winter. Since then, the Wildfowl Trust has welcomed a growing number of Bewick's each year. Over 600 winter at Slimbridge and nearly 3000 at Welney on the Ouse Washes in Norfolk.

The Wildfowl Trust's Centres (see opposite) offer both refuges for wild birds and collections of tame waterfowl. These are open daily to visitors. The Trust carries out research, conservation and education work at the Centres.

Membership is open to everyone interested in the aims and work of the Trust. There are supporter schemes which help towards the research and conservation programmes: you may "adopt a duck", "support a swan" or "support a Barnacle Goose"

For further details write to:
The Wildfowl Trust
Slimbridge
Glos. GL2 7BT

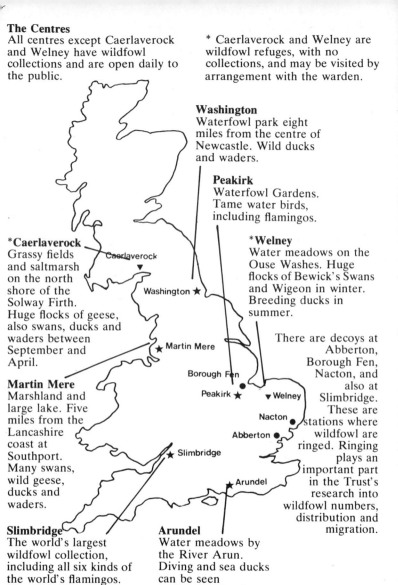

The Centres
All centres except Caerlaverock and Welney have wildfowl collections and are open daily to the public.

* Caerlaverock and Welney are wildfowl refuges, with no collections, and may be visited by arrangement with the warden.

Washington
Waterfowl park eight miles from the centre of Newcastle. Wild ducks and waders.

Peakirk
Waterfowl Gardens. Tame water birds, including flamingos.

*Caerlaverock
Grassy fields and saltmarsh on the north shore of the Solway Firth. Huge flocks of geese, also swans, ducks and waders between September and April.

*Welney
Water meadows on the Ouse Washes. Huge flocks of Bewick's Swans and Wigeon in winter. Breeding ducks in summer.

There are decoys at Abberton, Borough Fen, Nacton, and also at Slimbridge. These are stations where wildfowl are ringed. Ringing plays an important part in the Trust's research into wildfowl numbers, distribution and migration.

Martin Mere
Marshland and large lake. Five miles from the Lancashire coast at Southport. Many swans, wild geese, ducks and waders.

Slimbridge
The world's largest wildfowl collection, including all six kinds of the world's flamingos. Many wild swans, geese (including White-fronted) and ducks in winter.

Arundel
Water meadows by the River Arun. Diving and sea ducks can be seen underwater in clear pools. Also waders.

Caerlaverock ▼
Washington ★
★ Martin Mere
Borough Fen
Peakirk ★
▼ Welney
Nacton ●
Abberton ●
★ Slimbridge
★ Arundel

Threats to bird life

Pollution

Oil spills are all too frequent, polluting the sea and beaches and causing death to thousands of sea birds each year. Waste products from industry are still allowed to drain into rivers and streams. This type of pollution is a particular problem in estuaries.

More and more farmers use chemicals on crops to kill weeds and insects and to fertilize the soil artificially. These chemicals then seep from the land into ditches, streams and eventually rivers, poisoning plant and animal life. For example if a heron feeds for some time on fish it has taken from water continually polluted with insecticide, it may die. If it lives, the poisons which build up in its body prevent it from breeding.

Destruction of vital habitats

Even more species are threatened by people destroying or altering wetlands for the purposes of farming, industry or recreation. Water meadows, marshes, reed beds and lakes are being drained, rivers turned into canals, and salt-marshes and estuaries drained or reclaimed to provide more land.

Disturbance

Even habitats left in their natural state can be made useless to birds and animals by human disturbance, for example motorboats on lakes and rivers. This is especially true for birds during the nesting season and, for migrating birds like waders, during the spring and autumn. This is the time when they need to feed and rest for as long as possible before setting out on the next stage of their flight.

Good news

The efforts of organizations set up to conserve habitats and protect threatened species have meant that some species have now returned to Britain to breed. Some examples are the Avocet, Osprey and Black-tailed Godwit.

Humans have accidentally created some habitats which benefit certain birds. Reservoirs are good wintering places for wildfowl, and disused and flooded gravel pits attract birds like Great Crested Grebe and Little Ringed Plover.

What can you do to help?

Firstly, never disturb birds even to get closer to identify them. This is especially true during the nesting season, when disturbance may cause birds to leave the nest: their eggs may then be taken and eaten by other birds and animals.

Take special care on sea beaches during the nesting season. The eggs of terns and waders are well-camouflaged on sand and shingle and are therefore easy to tread on by mistake.

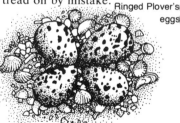

Ringed Plover's eggs

You can give your support by joining one or more of the organizations in the fields of conservation. Your membership fee will then be spent on efforts to help wild birds and conserve their habitats. See page 60 for addresses.

Glossary

Breeding season – the time of year when a pair of birds mate, build a nest, lay eggs and look after their young.

Colony – a group of birds of the same species nesting close together.

Colour phase – birds with two colour phases are identical in every way but found in two different coloured plumages.

Courtship display – when a male bird attracts a mate. Some birds show off their plumage. Others put on a "display" in the air. Some do both.

Dabbling ducks – a group of ducks which feed by dabbling in shallow water. Some "upend", i.e. turn upside down in the water with their tail ends and feet sticking up, to feed on water plants.

Diving ducks – a group of ducks which feed by diving for food underwater.

Eclipse – see moult.

Habitat – particular type of place inhabited by a bird or other animal, e.g. seashore, cliffs, freshwater.

Juvenile – a young bird which has left the nest and whose plumage is not yet the same as its parents'.

Migration – the regular movement of birds from one place to another, usually from the breeding area to the area where they spend the winter. Migrating birds are called migrants or visitors.

Moult – when birds shed their old feathers and grow new ones. All birds do this at least once a year. In ducks the duller plumage that remains during its moult is called *eclipse* plumage.

Passage migrant – a migrating bird is said to be on passage, and is called a passage migrant, when it is seen passing through one area to another. Passage migrants are usually seen in spring or autumn, on their way to breeding or wintering grounds.

Race or sub-species – two or more forms of the same species, but different in some ways such as in colour or size. They usually live and breed in different places. They can cross-breed.

Resident – a bird which remains all year in the area in which it nests.

Roost – to sleep. A roost is a place where birds sleep.

Species – a type of bird. For example Herring Gull is the name of one species in a group of birds called gulls.

Wildfowl – a collective name for ducks, geese and swans.

Books to read

A Colour Guide to Familiar Sea and Coastal Birds. Jiri Felix (Octopus).
A Colour Guide to Familiar Marshland and Freshwater Birds. Jiri Felix (Octopus).
Water and Shore Birds (Chatto Nature Guides). Walter Thiede (Chatto & Windus).
Birds of Sea and Coast. Lars Jonsson (Penguin).
Birds of the Inland Waters and Marshes. (Jarrold).
Birds of the Coast. (Jarrold).
Ducks, Geese and Swans. Oscar J. Merne (Hamlyn).
*Swans. Peter Scott and the Wildfowl Trust (Michael Joseph).
*Wild Geese. Myrfyn Own (Macmillan).
*Wildfowl of Europe. Myrfyn Own (Macmillan).
*Ducks of Britain and Europe. M.A. Ogilvie (T & A.D. Poyser).

*Waders (New Naturalist series) W.G. Hale (Collins).
*Seabirds, their biology and ecology. Bryan Nelson (Hamlyn)

General bird books
Collins Guide to Bird Watching. R.S.R. Fitter (Collins).
A Field Guide to the Birds of Britain and Europe. R.T. Peterson, G. Mountford & P.A.D. Hollom (Collins).
Book of British Birds. (AA/Reader's Digest).
Usborne Guide to Birds. Rob Hume (Usborne).
Bird Watching on Estuary, Coast and Sea. Clare Lloyd (Severn House).
*The Bird Watcher's Guide to the Wetlands of Britain. M. A. Ogilvie (Batsford).

*More advanced books

Useful addresses

Royal Society for the Protection of Birds (RSPB): The Lodge, Sandy, Beds.
Young Ornithologists' Club (YOC): address as for RSPB.
British Trust for Ornithology (BTO): Beech Grove, Tring, Herts.
Royal Society for Nature Conservation (RSNC): The Green, Nettleham, Lincoln, Lincs. This is the parent body for all county naturalist trusts. Also has a junior organization called WATCH. Most county naturalist trusts have a WATCH club. For more details write to RSNC.
Acorn Club (The Junior Division of the National Trust): The Old Grape House, Cliveden, Taplow, Maidenhead, Berks.
NB: When writing for advice or help of any kind, remember to enclose a stamped addressed envelope of a suitable size for your answer.

Scorecard

The birds are in alphabetical order. When you go spotting, put the date at the top of a blank column and, in the same column, fill in the score for each bird you see. At the end of the day, put your total score at the foot of each page. Then add up your grand total.

Species (name of bird)	Score	Date	Date	Date	Species (name of bird)	Score	Date	Date	Date
Avocet	25				Gannet	20			
Bittern	20				Garganey	25			
Bunting, Reed	15				Godwit, Bar-tailed	20			
Carolina Duck	15				Godwit, Black-tailed	20			
Coot	10				Goldeneye	20			
Cormorant	15				Goosander	20			
Crane	25				Goose, Barnacle	20			
Curlew	15				Goose, Bean	25			
Dipper	15				Goose, Brent	20			
Diver, Black-throated	20				Goose, Canada	10			
Diver, Great Northern	25				Goose, Greylag	15			
Diver, Red-throated	20				Goose, Pink-footed	20			
Dunlin	10				Goose, Red-breasted	25			
Eagle, White-tailed Sea	25				Goose, Snow	25			
Eider	15				Goose, European White-fronted	20			
Eider, King	25				Goose, Greenland White-fronted	20			
Egret, Great White	25				Goose, Lesser White-fronted	25			
Egret, Little	25				Grebe, Black-necked	25			
Ferruginous Duck	25				Grebe, Great Crested	15			
Flamingo, Greater	25				Grebe, Little	15			
Fulmar	15				Grebe, Red-necked	25			
Gadwall	20				Grebe, Slavonian	20			
Total					**Total**				

Species (name of bird)	Score	Date	Date	Date	Species (name of bird)	Score	Date	Date	Date
Greenshank	15				Peregrine	20			
Guillemot	15				Petrel, Storm	20			
Guillemot, Black	20				Petrel, Leach's	25			
Gull, Black-headed	5				Phalarope, Grey	25			
Gull, Common	15				Phalarope, Red-necked	25			
Gull, Great Black-backed	15				Pintail	20			
Gull, Herring	5				Plover, Golden	15			
Gull, Lesser Black-backed	10				Plover, Grey	15			
Harrier, Marsh	25				Plover, Kentish	25			
Heron, Grey	10				Plover, Little Ringed	20			
Heron, Night	25				Plover, Ringed	15			
Heron, Purple	25				Pochard	15			
Heron, Squacco	25				Pochard, Red-crested	20			
Kingfisher	20				Puffin	20			
Kittiwake	15				Rail, Water	15			
Knot	15				Razorbill	15			
Lapwing	10				Redshank	10			
Long-tailed Duck	20				Redshank, Spotted	15			
Mallard	5				Ring-necked Duck	25			
Mandarin Duck	15				Ruddy Duck	20			
Merganser, Red-breasted	20				Ruff	20			
Moorhen	5				Sanderling	15			
Osprey	25				Sandpiper, Common	15			
Oystercatcher	15				Sandpiper, Purple	15			
Total					Total				

Species (name of bird)	Score	Date	Date	Date
Scaup	15			
Scoter, Common	15			
Scoter, Surf	25			
Scoter, Velvet	20			
Shag	15			
Shearwater, Manx	20			
Shelduck	15			
Shoveler	15			
Skua, Arctic	20			
Skua, Great	20			
Smew	20			
Snipe	15			
Spoonbill	20			
Stilt, Black-winged	25			
Stork, Black	25			
Stork, White	25			
Swan, Bewick's	20			
Swan, Mute	5			
Swan, Whooper	20			
Teal, American Green-winged	25			
Teal, European Green-winged	15			
Teal, Blue-winged	25			
Total				

Species (name of bird)	Score	Date	Date	Date
Teal, Marbled	25			
Tern, Arctic	15			
Tern, Black	20			
Tern, Common	15			
Tern, Little	20			
Tern, Sandwich	20			
Tufted Duck	10			
Turnstone	15			
Wagtail, Grey	20			
Warbler, Reed	15			
Warbler, Sedge	15			
Whimbrel	20			
White-headed Duck	25			
Wigeon	15			
Wigeon, American	25			
Woodcock	15			
Total				

Grand Total			

Index